QUICK
Affirmations
FOR SUPER BUSY
MEN

A TO Z OF EASY PICK-ME-UPS
FOR NOT-SO-EASY DAYS

Written by
Yobe Qiu and Kim Ann

Illustrated by
Nejla Shojaie

This book belongs to:

_____

To our husbands,

Jason and Abe.

Your strength, determination, and focus have inspired us to create this project.

We appreciate your dedication to our families and your willingness to always be helpful.

Love, Yobe & Kim

Welcome!

Confidence, empowerment, and positivity are only a page away.

It's no secret that life can be challenging. With the right tools to help, you can develop a mindset that enables you to use challenges as opportunities to grow. Remind yourself of happiness and positivity, leaving negative perspectives behind you.

We are two entrepreneurs who know what it's like never to have enough hours in a day and know some days are not-so-easy. When it rains, it pours. But - we understand how important it is to develop a strong, positive growth mindset.

Using positive affirmations, it's possible to build confidence and strive toward success. You can revolutionize your approach to life and become the best version of yourself.

That's why we've written this book, providing you with a collection of A-to-Z affirmations that promote growth and personal development.

In this book, you'll find affirmations created with bold and ambitious men in mind. Read them regularly and begin to incorporate them into your daily life.

We hope this book helps you learn to think positively and pursue abundance.

Happy reading!

Yobe & Kim

I AM

Appreciated

AND

Accepted.

I AM
Balanced
AND Bold.

I AM
Confident,
IN CHARGE, AND
Conscientious.

I AM
Destined
AND
Determined.

I
Exceed
Expectations
OF MYSELF.

I AM

Focused

ON MY

Future.

I AM
Genuine
AND
DESTINED FOR
Greatness.

I AM *Heroic* AND *Helpful* TO OTHERS.

I AM

Important,

INSIGHTFUL,

AND

Influential.

I AM

Knowledgeable

AND SHARE

THAT KNOWLEDGE.

I AM
Loyal,
LEVEL-HEADED,
AND A
Leader.

I AM

Motivated,

MAGNETIC,

AND

Magnificent.

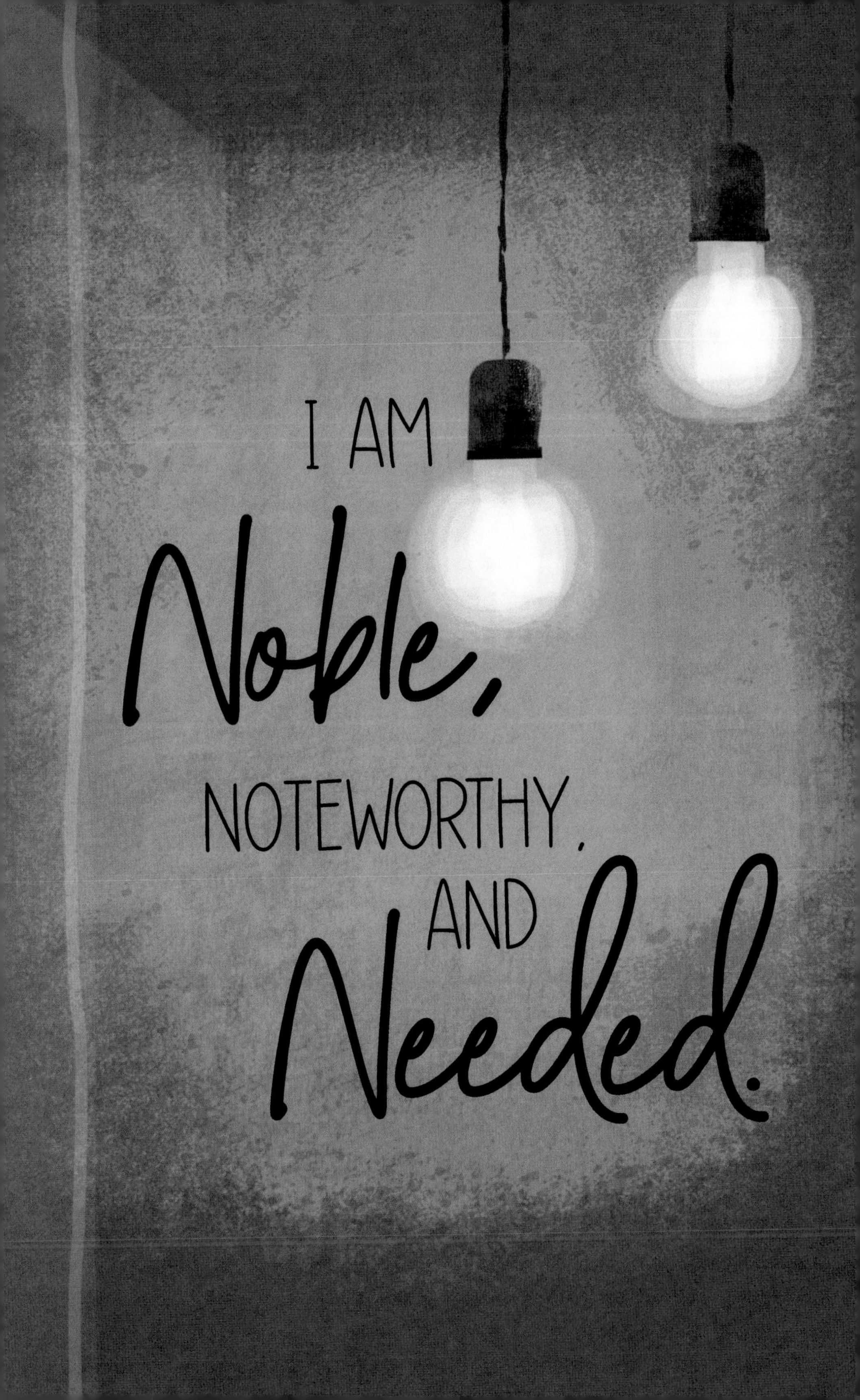
I AM
Noble,
NOTEWORTHY,
AND
Needed.

I AM
Optimistic,
OPEN-MINDED,
AND
One-of-a-kind.

I AM
Praiseworthy,
A PROVIDER,
AND
Proud
OF WHO I AM.

I AM *Quality* AND ENJOY MY *Quest.*

I AM

Resilient

AND A

Rock FOR THOSE

I LOVE.

I AM
Successful
AND
Substantial.

I AM

Trustworthy

AND

Thoughtful.

I AM

Unbeatable

AND

Unique.

I AM A
Visionary
AND CREATE
MY
Victories.

I AM *Wonderful* AND *Worthy.*

I AM

Xenial

AND

Xenacious.

I AM *Young* IN MY THOUGHTS AND *Yearn* TO KEEP GROWING.

I AM *Zen*
AND I AM AT PEACE.

Affirmations

_____

_____

_____

_____

_____

_____

_____

_____

_____

_____

_____

_____

_____

_____

_____

_____

Affirmations

_____

_____

_____

_____

_____

_____

_____

_____

_____

_____

_____

_____

_____

Affirmations

_____

_____

_____

_____

_____

_____

_____

_____

_____

_____

_____

_____

_____

_____

_____

Made in the USA
Middletown, DE
18 March 2023

27058429R00020